Responsible Decisions

by

E. David Cook

Lecturer in Philosophy and Ethics at St. John's College, Nottingham

GROVE BOOKS

BRAMCOTE   NOTTS.

CONTENTS

Page

Copyright E. David Cook 1974

First Impression November 1974

ISSN 0305 4241
ISBN 0 901710 58 X

INTRODUCTION

In the present climate of opinion, the emphasis is very much on demanding one's rights. Workers, management, pupil, teacher, shopper, shopkeeper, all are concerned to have their rights considered and catered for. They will defend their rights by every means possible. Strikes, violence, boycott, lockout, working-to-rule, all are legitimate tools in the support of one's claims. Responsibility talks not only of the rights of man, though it shouts these out in a very loud voice, but it also talks firmly of the obligations of man. There are no rights without obligations.

Each of us has certain basic rights which belong to us, but we also live in a web of responsibility. At home, work, in church, and as father, son, employer, employee, church leader or churchgoer, we are all responsible to others for certain things and they are responsible to us for other things. To be responsible may mean a variety of things: to be liable to be called to account; to be morally answerable for our actions; to be of good credit and repute. When we talk of being trustworthy, reliable and answerable or their opposites, we are dealing with responsibilities and our attitude towards them. In a whole variety of situations, with many different people, we are involved with different levels of responsibilities. The one who copes appropriately is responsible; those who fail—irresponsible.

One concern of the new Grove Books series on Ethics is to present an evangelical comment on central moral and theological issues of today, e.g. abortion and divorce.[1] There has also been felt a need for some direct writing on the foundational issues of ethics both as a stimulus for further Christian thinking and as a statement of a Christian outlook. This booklet falls into this category. It is an attempt to introduce some of the key ideas in responsibility both in an ethical and theological sense. It is intended as a basic introduction which gives an outline of some of the ways in which Christians can think more intelligently and informedly about responsibility and how it ought to affect themselves and their faith both as individuals and as a community. This means that when 'responsibility' is used in the booklet, Christian responsibility is meant. There is no attempt to argue for the Christian view or its adoption, but rather a brief statement of an approach to Christian responsibility.

As people read, the hope is that they will realise that they know far more than they realise about responsibility. Responsibility is no abstract, philosophical concept but part and parcel of our everyday life and action. Thus part of the aim of the booklet is to encourage further thought by the reader himself and in group settings about what we are responsible for, what limits there are to such responsibilities and how we face up to and cope with them. The latter part of the booklet seeks to explore some ideas in a tentative way, not as an end product, but hopefully as a stimulus to discussion, thought and action on the part of others, as they work through what christian responsibility is for twentieth century believers.

---

[1] See Booklet on Ethics no. 1—O. O'Donovan *The Christian and the Unborn Child*——and Booklet on Ethics no. 2—Franklyn Dulley *How Christian is Divorce and Remarriage?*

1. CHRISTIAN RESPONSIBILITY

Before analysing some different levels and situations of responsibility, we need to be clear about the fundamental nature of being responsible. This will involve seeing how responsibility has its proper setting in community. It is part of the basic fabric of society. It refers to intelligent, moral action. It stems from the motion of response, and its structure is essentially seen in the two ideas of being responsible *to* and being responsible *for*.

Responsibility is a mark of human life in community. If there was no community, there would be no responsibility, for responsibility assumes some sort of relationship. Responsibility binds people together in relationships to each other. The Jewish people were bound together by their choice by God, which meant that they had responsibility to God to behave as his chosen people. This responsibility was towards God and each other. It is in the Covenant relationship that God stresses mutual responsibility, which means that he takes on responsibility towards the Jews to be their God, and they to be his people. The Covenant responsibility had one expression in the Decalogue, where the demands and standards God required for his people had expression. The relationship to God of giving him his rightful place and serving him alone had priority over relations with one's fellowmen. There were clear rules for responsibility towards neighbours and these rules laid stress on the outward expression of attitudes as well as the inner quality of life. The commandments were the regulating principles of the whole of life as it was to be lived in relation to others, both God and mankind.

The kind of responsibility bound up in the Decalogue soon moves away from the formal societal commands and pressures into the realm of the habitual and apparently instinctual. We interiorise the rules and customs of the society in which we live. Our response to persons, actions and events takes for granted many responsibilities, which have become part of us even without our conscious knowledge. This level of responsibility is so basic that if we could remove it, chaos would result. In fact, we cannot remove it, for there is no way of easily expressing what life without such a fabric of responsibility would be like, far less trying to live it. An example will help. In our conversations we assume that people use words in the same way as we do, and that they mean what they say, and say what they mean. When we enter into conversation with someone, we trust them in the sense that we take what they say seriously and to some extent literally. We do have a system of checks, when people are likely to be lying, cheating, misleading or joking, but generally speaking we accept at face value what is said unless there is some reason to do otherwise. We assume that people are behaving responsibly in the way they use language. If we acted irresponsibly in our use of language once or twice, it might be taken as a joke (hence the stress on linguistic jokes, e.g. the pun); but to do so all the time would not only grate, but mean the collapse of communication by means of language. If we were no longer sure of what others were saying, we would soon be forced to retreat into the realm of private language, which Wittgenstein showed was no real tool of communication.[1] Responsibility about things like language use are part of the basic fabric of every society.

1 L. Wittgenstein *Philosophical Investigations* § 269, 275.

Commonly, however, there is a more usual meaning of responsibility. This relates to taking life seriously and acting in an intelligent and moral way. It is something more than emotions, for it is exercised whether we like it or not, and whether we want it or not. To neglect such responsibility may also bring a sense of guilt or remorse. When Peter, after all his impetuous boasting, betrayed Christ three times and then the cock crew, his tears were surely tears of remorse and guilt. When Christ had warned his disciples that all would leave him in his dark hour, Peter had recognised the responsibility of Christ's followers to follow him everywhere regardless of danger. His affirmation of loyalty was reaffirming his responsibility as a disciple of Christ to follow regardless. But the actual situation proved too much for Peter as it often does for all of us, and he betrayed Christ three times, failing in his responsibility to confess Christ as his leader. So often we are equally guilty of failing to confess our allegiance to Christ, when we too fail to respond to the opportunity and need of the situation.

This notion of responsibility stems from the idea of *response*. Man is able to do more than react, he can respond. He can answer for himself and his actions. He is answerable. He can reply, defend himself, give an account of himself and of his actions. In the Genesis narrative, when the fruit had been taken, Adam answers God, defending himself by blaming Eve and then God himself. 'It was the woman', was Adam's first line of defence. The real sting comes in the tail of his remarks. 'It was the woman *you gave me.*' Adam responds to the questioning of God, or rather to being called in question by God, by defending himself against the question. He is conscious of himself as a responsible agent with knowledge, will and capacity to answer for what he does. Even his refusal to accept blame by pointing the finger at someone else shows that he realised that blame is appropriate to someone. Adam is denying that he is that someone this time. Tacitly, he is accepting that if things had been different, he might well have been to blame. This leads us to the two-fold structure of responsibility.

The basic structure of responsibility may be seen in these two notions: being responsible *to* and being responsible *for.* We are responsible *to* both people and institutions. We are answerable to them. We are liable to be called to account by them. We recognise the need to give an account of ourselves, if we are questioned or queried. The worker is responsible to the management. The management is responsible to the shareholders. In situations of industry, commerce, military affairs, in other words, wherever there is a hierarchical structure of worker-manager, ruler-ruled, leader-follower, it makes sense to ask who is responsible and to whom, who is liable to be called in question, and who has the right to call this person to answer to them. We are responsible *to* people and institutions.

We are also responsible *for* people and things, but in this sense we are not answerable *to* those same people or things, instead we deputise for them. We take them under our protection and care and make ourselves answerable (responsible) for them. We act in their stead and on their behalf. This kind of responsibility is most clearly seen in the case of a parent's or guardian's responsibility *for* a minor. The parent is responsible for the child, for what he does, for exercising proper control over him or her. If the child does get into trouble, the parent is answerable *for* the child. In legal matters, he acts in the place of the child and on their behalf. He writes the cheques, makes the decisions or acts as proxy for the child.

In the story of Joseph, when he has still kept his identity from his family on their first visit and insisted that they bring back Benjamin to Egypt, if they want more grain, Jacob, the father, is unwilling to let his son go. In the midst of the argument, one of the brothers—Judah—makes himself responsible *for* Benjamin *to* Jacob. He is responsible *for* Benjamin. He deputises for him. He takes him under his protection and care. He agrees that if it is necessary he will act in Benjamin's place. He will stand proxy for Benjamin. At the same time he is responsible *to* Jacob (Genesis 4.3). He accepts that he is answerable to Jacob for whatever happens to Benjamin. He recognises that if it is necessary to answer any question, he, Judah, must give an account of himself and how he has exercised his responsibilities for Benjamin.

One sadly diminishing feature of our present society is the way in which we are tending to lose our sense of responsibility for each other. Older children often felt and were made responsible for their younger brothers and sisters. Because of their greater maturity and experience, they were expected to keep the younger ones from getting into mischief and trouble, and if they failed to do this then their parents did some imprinting of the hand to the seat of the pants. They had failed to behave in a sensible way, i.e. in an intelligent and moral way.

We must note that we are responsible *only* to those who have the right to call us in question', and to whom we are under some obligation to respond, or answer to and for. The manager of a rival firm has no right to complain to a worker from another company that his work is not up to standard. The worker is not responsible *to* that manager. The responsibility he has *for* a piece of work is not to be called in question by anyone except his own manager. The worker is responsible only for what he is contracted to do, nothing more and nothing less. In one sense, Adam was making a response which made very good sense in that he was trying to deny that he was the one to be called in question. He was saying it is Eve, or, for that matter, God himself, who is responsible for what has happened.

Very often a question can be dealt with by asking what right the person who asks the question has in the situation. Not everyone has the right to call us in question for what we do. A parent has more right to correct a child than a stranger, though we might wish that more strangers took their responsibilities to children more seriously. The problem here is of being told to mind your own business, either or both by the child and his parents. We may limit responsibility by questioning those who themselves call us in question as to their rights and interest in the matter.

In consideration of responsibility, it is important to realise that the Christian has responsibility for much that appears to be none of his business. There are few limits to what he is responsible for, not because he is a 'nosey-parker' who is always minding everyone else's business, but because in his responsibility *to* God, he discovers that he is responsible *for* far more than he imagines. Our responsibility stems not so much from these people *to* and *for* whom and those situations in which we have responsibility, but from our relation to God. If the root meaning of responsibility is that of response, the Christian life is a model for responsibility. The Christian is addressed and claimed by God. He is called in question by God as a sinner, as a created being who has fallen short of God's standard of living and he responds to God. The Christian response is the Christian life. It is the recognition that we are responsible to God for everything. This transforms the understanding we have of our responsibilities to and for others and things. My relation to creation, my fellow-man, my family, my work, my employer, and myself are all interpreted in terms of my response to God. I am called to live out the life of God by the power of the Holy Spirit, and so there is a clear hierarchy of responsibilities for the Christian. His responsibility to God always comes first, and because of such responsibility the Christian begins to love his brothers and sisters, his neighbours and his enemies as Christ did and because Christ did. Accordingly, the Christian has responsibility for much that is none of his business, simply because it is God's business.

One way of expressing how God's business is the Christian's business, is the idea of the Christian acting as God's deputy. In the situation where God is not visible, the Christian is God's visible deputy. One strong theme in the parables of Christ is that of the lord who goes off into a far country and leaves his servants to deputise for him. They are to act in his stead and on his behalf. They represent him and his interests in his absence. The Christian is God's deputy in two senses. He is first of all made in the image of God and as part of God's handiwork he reveals something of the nature of the Creator. He bears a family likeness, so that looking at the Christian one ought to be able to see a resemblance to the Father. One may gain a picture of the Father by looking at the image in his creature. The Christian is also a servant of the living God. He is a member of the people of God and is one for whom Christ died. As made in the image of God and as a servant of God, the Christian is responsible to God for what he does and how he lives. He is also responsible *to* others for *God,* in that he takes the place of God as far as they are concerned at least. What he says represents what God says. What he does: what God does. We are ambassadors for Christ in that wherever we are, whatever we say, and however we act, this is, in one sense, Christ in that situation.[1] Hence the force of the moral precept: 'Would Christ do this?' as a test for how we behave. This only makes sense if we are seeking to bring Christ to the situation or seeking to please Christ. That is the Christian's role as salt, light and leaven.

Responsibility is essentially responsibility *to* and responsibility *for*. It is response *to* and *for* persons, situations, and things. It is a life of being answerable and of deputising as an answer for someone else.

[1] The trap for Christians to avoid is thinking that everything depends on us. We take on ourselves the responsibility *of* God rather than the responsibility *for* God. He is the sovereign, responsible One, but as his deputies we are given responsibilities and we are called to be faithful in the little things as well as the great. We are called to deputise *for* him, but that does not necessarily mean that we are his only deputies or witnesses in any situation. To think we are is to try to take on the responsibility *of* him, rather than *for* him.

2 RESPONSIBILITY AND BLAME

The structure of responsibility is the *to* and *for* model. We are responsible *to* and *for* people and things. We showed that part of these senses of responsibility was the idea of being answerable for something to someone. There are occasions when we hold that people are answerable and others where we do not. Austin Farrer offers three features which must be present for a person to be held responsible in a situation. 1. *He could foresee the consequences.* 2. *He could have acted (or refrained from doing so).* 3. *He had a duty* (either to do or not do do it).[1] When one or more of these features is missing, we are aware of either irresponsible behaviour or of diminished responsibility. What we do when someone has behaved irresponsibly, is to blame or censure them. We point out where and how they have failed to do what they ought and what was reasonably expected of them. Such blame or censure is only justified if it is assumed that the other person could have acted responsibly. They must have been able to foresee the consequences of their action or inaction, to have been able to act or refrain from acting, and have had a duty to do or not to do it. There must have been no force or restraint used against them in any way so as to impair the responsibility.

One way of expressing the holding of a person as responsible is that he is free, or has freedom of the will. There is a close relation between the ideas of rationality and freedom. The rational person is the man who is free to make a reasonable judgment and to act upon it. There are two elements here. The one is that he has the capacity to make reasonable judgments without physical or mental hindrance or without any external force, let, or hindrance. The other is the ability to act, to do something, to exercise the decision made in a practical way. The responsible person is the one who is free to do otherwise because he sees the alternatives and could choose to do them, but instead fulfils his obligations and duties in a fitting manner.

In the situation where there is some physical or mental hindrance or some external force, we recognise that responsibility is impaired. We talk then of diminished responsibility. One clear set of examples of diminished responsibility centres on the cases of children and mentally defective people. They have no proper freedom of will because as yet they do not have what we count as free will. They are not yet able to make decisions which recognise all the aspects of the situation, and, therefore, do not respond appropriately to situations. The child has, as yet, no full and mature sense of will, so that his diminished responsibility is not so much that he is not free to do otherwise, but more that his will is not yet fully developed.

[1] A. Farrer *The Freedom of Will,* 'Responsibility and Freedom'.

This means that the child and the mentally defective person are unable to exercise full social or personal responsibility. They have no capacity to care for others in a way which is appropriate to them, e.g. there is a self-centred selfishness. There is no understanding of the exercising of prudence, foresight, or rationality. This means that a child does not realise fully the implications either of what may happen or the consequences which his own action may lead to. There is an inability to act appropriately to the needs of the situation and a lack of awareness of the impact of irresponsible behaviour. In other words, there is not sufficient experience of life or of situations to know what to do or how to proceed, and no means of weighing up likely outcomes. The difference between a child and a mature, responsible adult is that the child's expressions of shame, distress, remorse, or regret are not his own responses to a considered judgment of the situation and his failure to respond correctly, but rather a learned response from society or part of a moving towards a full adult response. The child himself does not appreciate why these responses are required and appropriate. Of course, this is not to say that every adult is perfect and every child totally inept in such situations. It is to say that there is a difference in the demands society and individuals make and expect from children to those expected from legally responsible, mature adults.

The other central area of diminished responsibility is where some external force or pressure removes this capacity to exercise full social or personal responsibility or by some means impairs it. This is the realm in the courts where the talk is not so much of criminal insanity, but of mitigating circumstances. Being carried away by one's emotions, being drunk, being under the influence of drugs, suffering from some kind of physical or psychological illness, and being brought up in a particularly difficult environment may all act as bases for suggesting that a person has diminished responsibility. In these cases, there would be little suggestion that this was an absolute thing, with no hope of improvement, otherwise a mental hospital or prison cell would appear to be the answer, where a public threat would be permanently(?) removed. Rather it would be an account of a particular instance, which was exceptional, which changed a mature, responsible person into an irresponsible actor in this case. It would not be part of a regular pattern, or else this would lead to a request for professional help from social workers, psychologists, or psycho-analysts.

These then are two areas where responsibility is neither claimed nor recognised, but some level of allowance made for those who cannot and do not exercise full social or personal responsibility. However, our language of guilt, shame, blame and distress, as with praise, desert and reward only makes sense if people are responsible for what they do and say or what they fail to do and say. If blaming someone made no difference, and if guilt were never experienced, these would be useless and meaningless terms, but they are used and are meaningful. This is not to say the everyone always feels them in the appropriate way, for some consciences grow hard, while others are over-sensitive.

Guilt, shame, blame, praise, reward and similar terms are related to liability. We all have obligations to different things. We are liable for our actions and decisions as parents, citizens, christians, colleagues, and workers. We accept and bear the consequences for what we have said and done, and what has been left undone in appropriate circumstances and situations. It is important to remember that this notion of accountability arises only when we have been called in question or when it is necessary to give reasons for what has happened. There is something peculiarly odd about the person who justifies himself when there is no call for or need to do so. There is a sliding scale of the reduction of responsibility and the reward or punishment for our behaviour, according to the degree of the mitigation of circumstances. Being carried away by emotions, being drunk, suffering from physical or psychological illness, being brought up in a particularly difficult environment may all mitigate the attitude taken towards someone who is called to account for his behaviour. There is also the interesting situation where we accept the responsibility; yet reject the blame. 'I acted in self defence', confesses the killer. He may then have the charge and penalty reduced to man-slaughter from murder. He admits that he did the deed, but wishes to change the description of the deed and its context. He admits responsibility for death, but not the death suggested by the original charge. Mitigating circumstances cast a different light on his behaviour.

It is also the case that for the Christian even if there is nothing explicit we can be held answerable for, that does not necessarily mean that we are all right in God's eyes. Perhaps Jesus was hinting at this when he suggested that even when we have done everything that is required, we are still unprofitable servants. Certainly we are responsible for more than simply our behaviour and speech. We are responsible for ourselves. One lesson of the Sermon on the Mount is that it is not just what we say and do, but also what we are 'inside', our motives, which matter. Our words and actions are taken as the expression of what we are. In some sense, we are what we do and say, and it is by our fruits we are to be known. Thus praising or blaming, rewarding or punishing is not done simply in relation to what we have said or done, but to ourselves as persons, who are responsible people. Responsibility is not just a feature of our actions and language, but of our beings.

Sin enters the picture in two particular ways. It is first of all the failure to fulfil all the responsibilities we know of. We are responsible for ourselves before God; for what we are, what we do and say, and what we think. We are answerable to God for every aspect of our life and how we use what has been given us. Sin is the failure to come up to God's standard. It is the failure to be free from question. We are all held accountable and all need to make answer. The Christian is the man who can both accept responsibility and live it out. This is not done in his own strength but it is done in the power which is given him in Christ. Jesus Christ is the model of man living out his responsibility before God. The Christian is called to imitate Christ and to fulfil his responsibility by his new life in Christ. Sin is, however, not just failure in being responsible, it is also the refusal to accept our right responsibility. Sin is more than falling short in our responsibilities; it is also falling short in being aware of how responsible we are—the extent of our responsibilities. We want to limit our responsibilities to those near and dear, to ourselves and to our own relations with God, but the man in Christ discovers that all of creation becomes his responsibility. The physical world, the animal kingdom, the whole of mankind belong to God, and the Christian takes his responsibility for these. This is not, of course, to say that he alone is responsible for all. He is responsible in partnership.

For the Christian, the thrill of becoming aware of his new extent of responsibility is that he does not, for indeed he could not, carry this burden alone. Christianity is partnership. It is primarily partnership with God, and then partnership with his people, the church. God is both the source of our responsibility and of the strength to face up to and successfully bear our responsibility. This takes the form, not of the isolated existentialist, but that of the organ of the body. The responsibility of the individual Christian is firmly grounded in the Christian community which shares his responsibility and supports him in it. The sovereign God is the one who supplies the power to face up to the extent and full weight of responsibility for the individual in community. If the Christian fails in responsibility either in carrying it through or realising its full scope, then blame and punishment are appropriate. But the joy of the Christian life is that forgiveness is the result of confession and repentance. The God who supplies both the responsibilities and the power to fulfil them, also is gracious and willing to forgive all who truly repent. If Christian responsibility is as great as we have been suggesting, then our cry is surely with Paul 'Who is sufficient for these things?' None of us is, and this is one way of expressing the penetrating effect of original sin. Here sin means that there is no possibility of exercising all our responsibilities appropriately both because of what we are and what the world is like. It is in this helplessness, we come to the forgiving God, who enables us to say, 'Our sufficiency is of God'. He is sufficient for our weaknesses, for his strength is made perfect in weakness. If our hearts and responsibilities condemn us, God is greater than both and enables us truly to repent. This true repentance involves facing up to the responsiblities, whether or not we feel like it, and whether or not we have in the past failed. This acceptance of responsibility is only possible in dependence on the power of the Holy Spirit, the gift of God.

3 RESPONSIBILITY IN SITUATIONS

Responsibility is a facet of community life and of personhood. Men are not islands. In every situation they are involved in, the situation is not so much an isolated pool as part of a continuous stream and flow of water. The present context only makes sense in relation to the past. When we enter a new situation, we ask ourselves what is going on there. The background of the situation is essential if we are to behave appropriately. We are liable to condemn the behaviour of those who act without thinking. Yet we are not so ready to condemn those who lack the relevant experience —the stranger in a strange land—or those who lack the powers of reasoning—the child or the mentally defective person. We can forgive social gaffes or childlike lack of inhibitions, but we expect the responsible person with experience and rationality to think through without negligence or prejudice the nature of the situation: its claims, its opportunities, the possible responses, and the attendant consequences.

We need to be clear that situations are not all of our own making. They are 'ongoing concerns' and we enter into a process of which we are but a part.[1] Many of our attitudes and views are not our own in the sense of thought through for ourselves, but are accepted without question from parent, priest, or politician. Hence responsibilities in social situations are both collective and individual. But these limitations do not undermine the picture we operate with of a rational man who is by his rationality, responsible. We still do and need to exercise our judgment in situations to observe, weigh up, evaluate motives, prospects and consequences, and to make a reasoned and reasonable decision which is appropriate. The key word here is *appropriate*. If the basic sense of responsibility is *response*, then the responsible person is the one who responds appropriately. He is the one who is able to meet properly the justifiable demands of situations and people. There is an old-fashioned expression which sums up appropriateness appropriately: 'It ain't fitting'. Appropriateness is what is fitting. Our response must fit the need, the situation, the demand, what is required and justified. Our response must be appropriate to the particular context, noting that in most situations there are multi-levelled contexts.

In other words, off-the-cuff reactions are inadequate unless they are firmly earthed in a clear grasp of the situation and its possibilities. We must use the intellect God has given us to weigh up the situation, as well as our wills and our emotions to respond to it as a whole person. It is essential to be clear about what is being said. It is *not* that each situation is itself and not some other situation, but rather that each situation is of a slightly different kind—a different blend of well-known ingredients—in which old attitudes have to be recombined and reapplied. Understanding the situation is the key and such understanding means recognising that there are different levels of needs, of responses, of awareness which need to be clearly separated. The doctor needs a clear *description* of a disease before he can offer the correct *prescription* for curing it. He needs to be

[1] W. H. Walsh, 'Knowledge in its Social Setting', *MIND*, 1971.

clear about its causes, its symptoms, its effects, its changes, and the ways of coping with it, before he decides which form of treatment to prescribe. Should we be any less concerned about our moral health?

Joseph was confronted with a pregnant Mary. A variety of contexts surrounded this situation. He was in love. He was engaged. He was a good and just man. He was aware of public reaction and desired to shield Mary from it. He had received a message from God and been addressed by the angel of the Lord. He made his appropriate response to the complex situation of the Virgin Birth (Matthew 1). He gladly took Mary as his wife. This kind of evaluation of the situation is both descriptive and prescriptive interpretation. In deciding what is the fitting response, we need to be clear what is in fact going on—description—and what ought to go on—prescription. When Paul talks of being all things to all men, he is talking of an appropriate response to different men with different needs. His goal is the same for all: to win them for Christ, but the steps taken towards that goal are flexible and not legalistic. At each point his concern is to fit the steps to the goal. Our response in social situations needs to be an appropriate one. We must use our God-given intellect to think through what the situation is, the needs involved in it, our role and our responsibilities, and the consequences of any and all actions or lack of them.

For the Christian, responsibility in each and every situation calls for him to use his God-given intellect to think through what God wants him to do in that situation. It is to be clear what the situation actually is and ought to be, and what the appropriate response is. The appropriate response means having the same mind as Jesus Christ. The appropriate response is the response which is appropriate to the Christian use of the mind, the Christian attitude towards the people and the situation and appropriate to what Jesus Christ would have done in the same kind of situation.

4 THE ORDERING OF RESPONSIBILITIES

It is not enough to know what our responsibilities actually are because sometimes responsibilities conflict with one another. In a recent class in ethics there was a debate concerning whether it was right to disobey an anti-christian government by smuggling Bibles into Czechoslovakia. Two, at least, of the principles in conflict were that of bringing the Good News to all nations and of being subject to all authority. The Christian, just as the non-christian, experiences conflict where responsibilities clash and contradict each other. Such conflict must happen and it is no wonder that it does when we remember that we live in a fallen world and we are fallen men and women. If this was the best of all possible worlds, then things might be so ordered that there was no conflict, no need for decision, no gap or difficulty in and between thinking what was right and doing it. But the world still awaits its full redemption. If we were the best of all possible people, then conflicts must disappear and we might know perfectly what is right and do it. We are, none of us, yet grown up into the fullness of the stature of Christ, and so there will always be conflict in deciding and fulfilling responsibilities, till that which is perfect is come.

A doctor who has a patient who is pregnant may have to decide between being honest with the mother about the danger of losing her child and adding psychological pressure to the physical pressures already existent, thus doing harm to the woman involved. When the nurses of a large hospital go on strike, how do we balance their low wages, difficult working conditions, unsocial hours, responsibility for patients, and length of training, against the needs of the patients and the needs of society? In such conflicts of responsibilities how are we to work out our own hierarchy of responsibilities? Which moral principles are to come first?

We need to be particularly careful because the way we describe a situation can, in fact, make a great deal of difference to it. If a doctor is asked to advise a patient on the subject of abortion, then to tell the mother that the doctor will scrape out the baby is liable to have quite a different effect from telling her that the doctor plans to evacuate the uterus. Such a loaded *description* comes very near to *prescribing* which order of moral principles will and ought to be followed. While we need not only to describe what the situation is, but also to *prescribe* what ought to be done in it, we must not cheat and beg the question by blurring the description with our own prescription: the situation, with our response to it.

In the understanding of a situation and the appropriate response to it, the need for descriptive and prescriptive interpretation has been stressed. It is not enough to know simply what is going on in any situation, we must also be clear what ought to happen. The facts of the situation need to be seen in relation to the morality of the situation. What moral principles are relevant? How do we apply them here? How do we resolve any conflict? These are the sorts of questions, which ought to be asked if the responsible man is not just intelligent, but also moral. Right and wrong need to be sorted out as much as the other parts of the situation. This inevitably leads to problems, as in the case of Joseph and the Virgin Birth, different moral principles conflict, and decisions between possible responses have to be made. As a husband-to-be, as a righteous man, as a man addressed by God, Joseph had to decide which responsibility came first. He exercised his judgment on the basis of an hierarchy of responsibilities.

To be fair to ourselves we must realise that the normal and habitual are just that. Normal and habitual. In most cases our responsibilities are clear. There is no easy escape from them without shutting our eyes to the obvious. Crucial issues of conflict are fewer and further between than most moral philosophers lead us to believe. For the most part, we know in any situation what we ought to do and which responsibility has priority. Having said that, however, there is at times tension between competing claims, and it seems, the more we think about it the harder the problem is to solve. Is my prime responsibility to myself, to my family, to my church, to my country, or to my God? If two of these come into conflict, which responsibility am I to concentrate on, and which allow to lapse, given that I can't do both? Often we can do both perfectly well, but it is the rarer situation where we cannot that must be faced. For the Christian there are two important steps. The first is common to all reasonable men, the other unique in its statement, if not in its procedure of selecting values.

When any reasonable person, who is not a child or in some way mentally defective, is confronted with a conflict of responsibilities or duties, the first step is to be clear as to what the conflict actually is. What is the back ground to the situation? What is the nature of the situation? What are the responsibilities involved? What are the possible responses? Which are the appropriate responses to the different responsibilities? What are the likely effects and consequences? In other words, *TO WHOM* and *FOR WHAT* am I responsible in this situation? What do I have to give an account for and to whom am I answerable here? It is only when we have answered these questions that we can actually make sense of the situation and be clear what responsibilities we actually have. In most cases this will be enough to clarify what we have to do. To have worked out what is involved in a situation, is often to see what is to be done. Certainly without such clarification we are less than rational and are in danger of being guided simply by reactions, emotions alone, or being simply irrational. This is not to belittle our reactions or emotions, nor to deny them a proper place, but rather to put them in the total context of what a man is—a thinking, willing, as well as a feeling, person. When Christ met the rich young ruler, we are told that he looked on him and loved him. But his response to the young man was not simply an emotional experience, it was to recognise the man's genuine need and to confront him with the real solution to his problems. That was, in his case, to give away his wealth to the poor and then to follow Christ. Our response to people and situations is more than how we feel about people and things. It is also what we think about them and how we will to act and speak towards them.

If the first step is to be clear about the responsibilities in any given situation, understood as far as is possible, the second step for the Christian, as for everyone, is to choose between responsibilities, when and if they conflict. Each person, in fact, functions with an hierarchy of responsibility which can be read back from what the person has done in past situations of conflict. The tutor who refuses to organise a meeting with a student at his family tea-time, is showing that his family tea-time is more important a responsibility to him than this particular student's query at that particular time. This is not to say that a particularly severe request or problem might not change the order of responsibilities, but that outwith[1] the college setting, family comes before students as a general rule. Particular cases might well mean exceptions, but the norm is family first, unless there is good reason.

Each of us, then, has a more or less explicit order of responsibilities which we use as a rule of thumb in deciding what we ought to do. But is our order the right one? How are we to decide between our responsibilities to and for our family, our neighbours, the poor in this country, and the starving abroad? If all men are my brothers, and I am my brothers' keeper, how do I cope with all the demands that this makes upon me and how do I decide between different responsibilities? The danger is of a retreat from all responsibility. Because there is so much need and I have so little to give, it is useless to do anything. Because we cannot do everything, we do nothing, rather than doing something. If the sheer number and extent of those suffering from malnutrition was the only factor, then to give anything is useless. It makes so little difference. But it does make some difference. If one person is fed, one need relieved, then part of the problem has been met. We need to act on the basis of doing what we can, rather than complaining because we cannot do everything.

If then, we try to face up to our responsibilities, how do we decide the order of priorities? The continuing debate between Jesus and the Pharisees may be viewed as a debate about the order of responsibilities. Jesus and the Pharisees were both religious in outlook. They were concerned about God and being right with him. They were concerned to do his will and to please him. The Pharisees had worked out one way of pleasing God. It was to keep all the commandments. Their concern was with avoiding what was wrong. It was to avoid being guilty by breaking the law. Unfortunately some of the laws were not explicit enough, so a supplementary commentary of man's own making had been added to clarify how the law could be kept and not broken. For example, the Sabbath was to be kept holy. The Pharisee then had thirty-nine rules for keeping the Sabbath. In healing the man with the withered hand on the Sabbath, Christ was calling their order of priorities into question. 'Is it lawful to do good on the sabbath or to do evil? To save life or to kill?' People in need matter more than rules and regulations in themselves. This is not to say that rules are irrelevant, but rather that, in a situation of conflict, the rules for the needs of man must come before keeping the rules for the rules' sake. To keep the rules for righteousness' sake is to be in danger of allowing one's love and concern for oneself to take priority over a proper love of others. Part of the Pharisees' problem was that the rules were not sufficiently widespread and ordered to

1 This preposition is the author's Scottish version of the English 'outside of' [Editor].

be a reliable guide to righteousness. The Sabbath was made for man, not man for the Sabbath. Christ was trying to show the Pharisees that in their desire to keep the law of God, they had substituted their own inadequate codification in place of the wider and more rigorous codification of Christ. Christ states that we have never finished loving our neighbours, or forgiving our brothers.

The same kind of questioning of priorities occurs in the parable of the Good Samaritan, both in the setting and in the content of the story. The victim of our 'mugging' is passed by the priest and the Levite. The Samaritan is the only one to stop and help. The priest and the Levite knew that they would be breaking the law if they touched someone who looked as if he were dead. But no law would be broken if they passed him by. Christ showed however that the law of loving one's neighbour was in fact broken. The parable is a judgment on the attitude of the priest and the Levite. It is also an affirmation of the lifestyle and practice of the Samaritan. The priorities of the priest and the Levite were wrong. So too were the priorities of the lawyer who baited Christ with, 'Who is my neighbour?' It is the Samaritan and not the priest or the Levite who has the divine perspective on things. He has the right hierarchy of responsibilities.

The Scribes and the Pharisees who opposed Christ were attacked not so much for their opposition to Christ, but for failing to distinguish between the essential and the inessential, the important matters of the law and the less important ones. 'Woe unto you Scribes and Pharisees, hypocrites! For you pay tithes of mint and anise and cumin and have omitted the weightier matters of the law, judgment, mercy and faith; these you ought to have done and not to have left the other undone. Blind guides, who strain at a gnat and swallow a camel' (Matt 23.23). The Pharisees had got things in the wrong perspective. It was important to give a tithe to God, recognising that everything came from him and belongs to him. But purity had come before charity instead of going along with it. The keeping of the minutiae of the law had led to the ignoring of the call of the prophets to aid the poor and needy. There could not be the one without the other. God's concern was not only for tithes and offerings, but rather for right action and genuine loving towards those who needed it. Justice and mercy ought to be manifested not just in the small personal details of a man's life, but in the broad sweep of his relationships with others.

In a marriage there is much more than a list of obligations and duties to be fulfilled. There is also a depth of love and concern, which transcends the keeping of rules, not by breaking them, but by fulfilling them and, indeed, going beyond what is required, because of love. Imagine staying in the home of a couple who had in the kitchen two lists. One list was for the husband, the other for the wife. Each list contained all the things that the other had to do if they were to show the reality of their love for their spouse. When, and only when, each of the items on the list had been fulfilled and ticked off, could it be said, 'He, or she, does love the other'. What a travesty of a marriage relationship! This surely reveals a complete misunderstanding of the nature and practices of love. If this is true concerning human love and the responsibilities it brings, how much more true will it be of human love towards the divine and the responsibilities such love brings.

The Pharisees had reduced the worship and obedience towards God to a cold, calculating, and rigorous exercise with little joy. The letter of the law was killing the reality of God in men's lives. Christ stopped the rot not by rejecting the law, but by fulfilling it. He showed in his life, actions, words, and most of all in himself, what was important for man to do. He showed what man's life in God was meant to be. He exemplified the correct relation of the created with the Creator. One correct interpretation of what Christ did in the Incarnation is surely to show man his responsibilities and the exercising of these responsibilities. This revelation of what man ought to do and could now do because of the new life of the kingdom, was of man's true responsibilities. The commandments can be summed up in two, 'Love God' and 'Love your neighbour as yourself'. These are the hallmarks of the kingdom. But Christ's precepts were not simply words. He alone could say 'Do as I do as well as what I say'. If we want to know what the responsibility to love God and to love our neighbour actually entails, we need look no further than the example of Christ. Christ shows us, in practice, the responsibilities on man and the order these ought to take.

The Christian is not only to follow the pattern of Christ's incarnate order of responsibilities, but to recognise that this is only possible by the full use of Christ's power for us and in us. Christ came to the lame man and said, 'Get up and walk'; to the bedridden, 'Take up your bed and walk'; to the man with the withered hand, 'stretch forth your hand'; to the dead, 'Come forth'. Christ made impossible demands on people. He commanded them to do the impossible: the very thing which they could not do. This only makes sense if with the command comes also the power to obey the command. This is the power which enables the lame to walk, the weak to carry their beds, the cripple to move the crippled limb, and the dead to rise. When Christ commands, he also provides the power to keep the command As we look at the demands on us and the need to follow the priorities of Christ we might well admit we are on a hiding to nothing. But Christ's power makes all things possible, if it is appropriated. But we need to say more about the priorities of Christ.

His ordering of responsibilities is seen in these main respects. At the general level, the Christian fulfils his responsibilities by living a life of total obedience before God. It is God's will which comes first in both the easy and hard things. In the garden, at Caesarea Philippi, on the cross, it is Christ's obedience in always doing those things which please the Father, which is to be the main priority of the Christian. To be like Christ, is to be obedient as he was. It is to seek God's will for oneself and then to do it gladly, because it is his will and because he knows best. More particularly, the order of responsibilities is embodied in the manifesto of the kingdom. The Sermon on the Mount is the manifesto of the kingdom in Matthew chapters five to seven. In this the questioning of the priorities of the Pharisees reached its height. The new responsibilities of life as a member of the kingdom are set against the old responsibilities as stressed by the Pharisees.

In Matthew 5.21, we read, 'You have learned how it was said to our ancestors: "You must not kill, and if anyone does kill he must answer for it before the court".' This is responsibility as defined by the Pharisees. Christ now adds to this, 'But I say this to you: anyone who is angry with his brother will answer for it before the court; if a man calls his brother, "Fool", he will answer for it before the Sanhedrin; and if a man calls him, "Renegade", he will answer for it in hell-fire'. Christ's standard of responsibility is far greater and deeper than that of the Pharisees. It sets an impossible standard, which man alone cannot keep; thus throwing man back on God rather than leaving him to his own devices. It gives priority to the inner, the secret acts and states, which lie behind the more explicit public acts and states. It shows that motives matter as much as actions. It reveals that need to get our attitudes right as well as the appearances. It stresses that the love of God and the law of God are more demanding, and require total commitment far beyond mere legalism. Christ's ordering of responsibilities is a call for a more radical, vibrant and costly discipleship than that of the Pharisees.

Matthew 5.27 follows the same formula. 'You have learned how it was said: "You must not commit adultery". But I say this to you: if a man looks at a woman lustfully, he has already committed adultery with her in his heart'. Christ's standard of sexual responsibility relates not just to the explicit action but the implicit attitude of mind. He continued to set out his new responsibilities for the member of the kingdom in verse 31. 'It has also been said: "Anyone who divorces his wife must give her a writ of dismissal". But I say this to you: Everyone who divorces his wife except in the case of fornication, makes her an adulteress; and anyone who marries a divorced woman commits adultery'. Again from verse 33 he stated 'Again, you have learned how it was said to our ancestors: "You must not break your oath, but must fulfil your oaths to the Lord". But I say this to you: Do not swear at all, either by heaven, since that is God's throne, or by the earth, since that is his footstool, or by Jerusalem, since that is the city of the great king'.

The same structure of setting the old responsibility against the new is continued twice more. 'You have learned how it was said: "Eye for eye and tooth for tooth". But I say this to you: Offer the wicked man no resistance' (verses 38-39). Then also in verses 43-44. 'You have learned how it was said: "You must love your neighbour and hate your enemy". But I say this to you: Love your enemies and pray for those who persecute you; in this way you will be sons of your Father in heaven, for he causes his sun to rise on bad men as well as good, and his rain to fall on honest and dishonest men alike.'

In all these verses we see two central things. Christ clearly states his opposition to the picture of responsibilities given by the Pharisees and over and against this picture, he offers his own new standards of responsibility which go far beyond the old ones in scope, motivation, and content. His priorities are now to be the priorities of the Christian, who lives the life of the kingdom. Christ's ordering of responsibilities is contained in the manifesto of the kingdom—the Sermon on the Mount.

For the Christian who wishes to be clear about the biblical order of responsibilities there is the general need to live a life of obedience to God, and, more particularly, to follow the themes of the manifesto of the kingdom. There is one further way of understanding Christ's hierarchy of responsibilities. This is contained in Matthew 25, which is set in a block of teaching about being ready for the Master, having the lamps filled with oil, using one's talents properly. It is accordingly meant to depict a judgment about the reality of christian profession for those who call Christ, 'Lord' rather than a standard for how others have treated Christians. The scene is Christ coming in glory and the subject is judgment. The sheep are separated from the goats. The standard for separation into one category or the other is repeated. Once the words are words of commendation. The other time the words are words of condemnation. Christ addresses the blessed on his right hand with, 'For I was hungry and you gave me food; I was thirsty, and you gave me drink; I was a stranger and you made me welcome; naked and you clothed me, sick and you visited me, in prison and you came to see me'. But his words and demeanour to those on his left are tragically similar yet with an eternal distinction. 'For I was hungry and you never gave me food; I was thirsty and you never gave me anything to drink; I was a stranger and you never made me welcome; naked and you never clothed me; sick and in prison and you never visited me'. What counts for eternity is not using the term 'Lord' to and of Christ, but feeding the hungry, relieving the thirsty, welcoming the stranger, clothing the naked, visiting the sick and imprisoned. This is part of the hierarchy of responsibility that Christ lays down for his disciples. It is worth noting that in Matthew's account, this statement of responsibility comes after and in the context of the parables of the conscientious steward, and of the wise and foolish virgins (bridesmaids), and of the talents. The Jerusalem Bible then translates the verse after the account of the Last Judgment as follows: 'Jesus had now finished all he wanted to say . . .' It is as if the responsibilities hammered home in the separation of the sheep and the goats are, as it were, part of the climax of Christ's teaching. He now sets his face to the cross. The last lesson is his death.

When considering our responsibilities, we need to clarify what are the actual responsibilities in the situation by examining what the situation is and thinking through the consequences of any action taken. However, if there is a conflict of responsibilities, we must not be afraid to act in accordance with the order of responsibilities which we operate with. For the Christian the hierarchy of responsibilities is not something he need decide from scratch. Christ has set out the responsibilities of the member of his kingdom in the Sermon on the Mount and in the account of the Last Judgment. But it would be too easy to imagine that Christ's order of priorities is simply another idealistic creed and to dismiss it accordingly. Christ not only propounded his view, he lived it. His hierarchy of responsibilities was incarnate in his person and work. Christ not only taught an example of the responsible life, he lived the example. The Christian then must equally let Christ's order of responsibilities become part of his flesh. He must do the work of Christ and fulfil the image of God. Insofar as we are like Christ, we have the order of priorities in our responsibilities, which is God's will for the Christian.

5 RESPONSIBLE DECISIONS—ASPECTS FOR DISCUSSION

In the major part of this booklet the theme has been to introduce something of the nature, extent, and content of responsibility for the Christian. It has been an attempt to link together philosophical and theological insights to form a coherent approach in order to offer a better understanding of what it means to be responsible. Part of the thesis has been that the whole of the Christian's life is a life of responsibility and that the Christian life is the responsible life, *par excellence*. There has been no attempt to argue for this against alternative views of responsibility, but rather the clarification of what such an assumption entails. The key to understanding what responsibility is rests on seeing that it stems from *response*. The responsible person makes a *fitting* response. It has been shown that the basic structure of responsibility is on the *to* and *for* model. The setting of responsibility in the context of a community was noted and the impossibility of using any other picture of responsibility. The major part of the booklet has concentrated on examining the problem of the ordering of responsibilities. The use of God's gift of reason was stated to be crucial in clarification of the situational aspects of our responsibilities and the appropriateness and fittingness of particular responses. It is necessary to be clear what is the nature of each situation, its background, the responsibilities involved, the possible and the likely consequences or results. It was claimed that such an analysis of what was actually involved in a situation would help clarify what ought to be done. It was admitted that situations do arise where there is a conflict of responsibility. For the solution to such conflicts, the example of Christ was crucial. His work, person and teaching provide the Christian order of responsibilities; and his priorities, guidelines for those who follow him.

Part of the purpose of clarifying the notion of responsibility for the Christian is not only to have a better idea of what responsibility is, but also and more importantly, to try to stimulate fellow Christians into thought and action as individuals and groups with some of the material involved. To facilitate this exercise, a number of key areas for thought will be presented. Each is a self-consistent theme: yet all are bound together by the theme of responsibility. These are meant to form the basis for thought and discussion, and to help others to develop for themselves what their responsibilities are and how, by the grace of God, they will fulfil them.

1. Responsibility makes sense only in the context of a community. It depends on the idea of *mutuality*. Each of us belongs as much to society and to each other as we belong to ourselves. Modern literature, art, and drama have misled us into the extreme individualism of Existentialism. Being a person has for too long been thought of as a characteristic of man alone, rather than of men in community. The inner aspects of personality have been stressed at the expense of the outer. We have tried to erect barriers between ourselves and others by talking of the inner world as if we lived inside ourselves, rather than living in the world.

   If Existentialism is wrong, then responsibility is not so much *mine* as *ours*. This means that I take responsibility for what my society is doing, e.g. pollution, economic exploitation, military aggression, corrupting the young. It also means that I am involved in the moral issues of the day. The doctor who has to decide who is to have a kidney machine and who is to have a transplant operation, when in both cases resources are limited, must not be left to carry the responsibility of decision making alone. As a member of society, I ought to be aware of the problem and helping in some way to solve it. That may mean becoming a kidney-donor, writing to the local hospital, or encouraging others to write about and think through the problem. We must learn to bear each other's burdens as well as our own. How can we share responsibility?

Given that responsibility is part and parcel of what we do as well as of our attitudes, do we show that we are responsible by the kinds of lives we live? Do our actions and words reveal our order of priorities more than we think? Are we growing as we face up to new levels of responsibility? How can we do the truth and better fulfil the extent and content of our responsibilities?

2. The Christian is a member of a group. He is a member of the church just as the Jew was a member of the chosen people of God. One difficulty of being a member of a group is that in belonging to others we do not necessarily choose them for ourselves. We enter into an ongoing institution with parts which were there before us and others which will be there after us. The Christian has no more choice in the matter of brothers and sisters in Christ than he does in his own natural family. As a Christian, he has responsibility not only to and for himself, that means to and for himself as a part of the body of Christ. As a Scot, I may be proud of Scotland's achievements in the World Cup, and equally, ashamed of the crime record of Glasgow. The interesting thing is that I neither played in the World Cup, nor have added to or subtracted from the total of crime in Glasgow. I am proud, feel ashamed, and have similar attitudes because I recognise that I am responsible for things I have no direct part in. My representatives increase the crime rate on a Saturday evening in Glasgow. Because I am a Scot and recognise my responsibility to my representatives and theirs towards me, I am entitled to shame and pride.

If this attitude is justifiable, then to what extent is the Christian responsible for his representatives? For what the Church does in Spain, South Africa, South America? How far does my responsibility go for my representative whose life is a sermon which no one ought to hear? Whom do I represent?

3. F. H. Bradley once commented 'What is duty? It is simply the other side of rights'.[1] In the present climate of opinion, the emphasis is very much on demanding one's rights. The worker ,the management, the pupil, and the teacher, all are concerned to have their rights considered and upheld. They will defend their rights by every means possible. Responsibility talks not only of the rights of man, though it shouts these out in a very loud voice; it also talks firmly of the obligations of man. There are no rights without obligations. The right to freedom of speech involves the obligation not to abuse that freedom and to defend it if it is in jeopardy. The right to a fair wage

1 F. H. Bradley, *Ethical Studies*, 'Rights and Duties'.

involves the obligation to earn that wage in return for a fair work.

Am I more interested in my rights, than in my obligations? What are my obligations? What are the limits of my duties? Do I recognise the obligations of others and encourage them to accept these duties for themselves?

4. It is right and proper to ask in a situation what are the responsibilities involved and how may one meet them. However, such a questioning must come to an end somewhere. If it is true that our responsibilities ought to become part of us, then analysis, questioning ,and searching for responsibilities ought to be an exceptional thing. The Christian life is not a life of constant questioning or stilted self-analysis, but rather a more relaxed life, in the sense of being a life full of grace, peace and joy. Our aim as Christians ought to be a life so guided by the Holy Spirit that our responsibilities as Christians become instinctive and natural and do not need to be thought through all the time, every time.

Do I question beyond the prompting of the Spirit and outwith the sovereignty of God?

5. Responsibility does not depend on my feelings. I am responsible whether I feel it or not, whether I like it or not. Relations exist whether I feel them or not. We are bound to God, to ourselves, to each other, whether or not we feel anything in particular. Moral insensitivity does not absolve us from responsibility. It merely reflects our failure in responsibility. There is little limit to the areas of responsibility for the Christian, and it often seems that the 'duties 'of super-erogation are the norm: going the second mile, turning the other cheek, loving one's enemies. We are not concerned as Christians with reciprocity. We ought to give and not to count the cost. To fight and not to heed the wounds, to labour and ask for no reward. The Christian is the one who does more than is required and who recognises no limit of group or community. The world is his oyster. Is it ours?

6. A right view of being responsible, inevitably includes responsibility to oneself. We must seek a right kind of self-development, which conforms us to the image of God. We are responsible to fulfil our own calling and to use our own gifts. Have we, are we, do we? Is one of our sins the refusal to accept our responsibilities?

7. Others have a call on the Christian, for in Christ, the Christian is responsible for others. He is his brothers' keeper. This means that the Christian is sensitive to two areas concerning others. He is sensitive to their needs and to their value. All men in need are part of our responsibility as Christians. Nevertheless, the Lazarus at the gate, the Macedonian who invites us over to help him, and the man lowered through the roof by his friends, are all examples of the need being there without any tortuous process of searching. Clearly the nearest needs deserve prior attention. How often does the plight of the refugee in Hindustan take precedence over that of the orphan in next street? Our neighbour is the person next to us who is in need.

Needs are not the only area of responsible sensitivity for the Christian to be aware of. Equally, the Christian accepts the value of persons; for

God created them and Christ died for them. If Christ died for the woman or man next door, how much am I required to do for them?

8. R. Niebuhr writes, ' . . . responsibility is not an extra, merely an element in life, but it constitutes our human life itself'.[1] All of life is responsibility. Every department of our lives carries responsibility. In creation, in covenant relationships, as sons and daughters, and as stewards, we have different levels of responsibility that have to be fulfilled. We are responsible to God, to his creation, to what he has done and is doing, and for what he has given us. There is nothing prior to our obligation to God, but we must beware of the same kind of legalism about responsibility as marked the lives of the Pharisees. They had no balance between rules and creativity. By creativity is meant the constant widening of the scope and practice of rules better to meet the needs the rules were designed for. The wonder of the person and work of the Holy Spirit is that while the letter may kill, the Spirit gives life. Under his inspiration, the Christian must seek creative ways of fulfilling responsibility. This is possible as long as a clear picture is kept of why we are responsible and the basis on which we accept responsibility. It is part of our response to God. He has taken the initiative. We respond to him, because he first addressed us and brought us into a new relationship with himself. Love so amazing, so divine, *demands* response to all that God desires.

The responsive life is the obedient life. How obedient am I?

9. In a very real sense, the responsible life cannot be taught, it can only be caught. The responsible life is a catching one. Bergson was fond of the idea that the responsible life could not be preached, but rather it showed itself, and its presence stirred others to action.[2] The impact of the saint and the hero is not so much the theses propounded in dogmatic form, but the quality of life lived. The full impact of Christ, is not in his teaching alone, but in the Word made flesh and dwelling among us so that his glory may be seen, that glory which is full of grace and truth. The best sermon on responsibility which can be preached is the practice of a responsible man or woman.

What message am I the medium of?

10. In his own tantalizing way Bonhoeffer wrote, 'The origin, essence, and goal of the responsible life is in Jesus Christ'.[3] For the Christian, nothing may be added and nothing taken away from Christ as the pattern of responsibility for us. He is the man for others. He is the servant of all. His life is poured out in love for others. We can have no other responsibilities than his, no other style of life than his, no other awareness of responsibility, nor power of fulfilment, than his. The responsible life is the Christian life: that is the life of Christ lived out by twentieth century man for the glory of God.

[1] R. Niebuhr, *The Responsible Self*, Chapter One.
[2] H. Bergson *Two Sources of Morality and Religion*, 'Moral Obligation'.
[3] D. Bonhoeffer, *Ethics*, 'The Structure of Responsible Life'.